Mike Read's
Rock and Pop
Quiz Book

ELM TREE BOOKS/LONDON
in association with Sphere Books

First published in Great Britain 1981
by Elm Tree Books/Hamish Hamilton Ltd
Garden House 57-59 Long Acre London WC2
by arrangement with BBC Publications Ltd

Distributed by Sphere Books Ltd

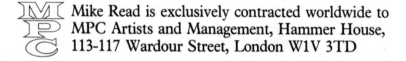 Mike Read is exclusively contracted worldwide to
MPC Artists and Management, Hammer House,
113-117 Wardour Street, London W1V 3TD

Jacket photograph by Beverly Lebarrow:
typography and design by Ken Reilly

Book design and typesetting by GMGraphics
Harrow-on-the-Hill, Middlesex
Printed and bound in Great Britain by
Richard Clay (The Chaucer Press) Ltd, Bungay, Suffolk

Contents

Acknowledgements
Thanks to the BBC for the photograph on pages 44/45. The photo on page page 10 is by Joe Faull; the top photo on page 21 by Joe Bangay; the one on page 38 by Neil Dalrymple; page 58 by John Timbers; page 63 by Allan Ballard; and page 77 by Flair Photography Ltd.

Well hi there!

Mike Read.

"If only you were knowledgeable about something *useful*!" a wise person once said to me. Ah, if only I'd listened, the BBC might never have asked me to do a TV Pop Quiz and I might never have been cornered in a dark alley by the Elm Tree boys and persuaded to write a book. But I didn't listen, so here is a collection of mini 'O' levels in pop that won't qualify you for anything, but should provide hours of fun and the opportunity to show off endlessly to your friends. And for real clever dicks, I've thrown in some samples of *Beat the Jock* questions from my Radio One Breakfast Show.

How much music does your dad remember from the days when he still had hair and played centre forward for the local team? How many of the 45s that your mum used to play in her bedroom or sing on the way to the local recreation ground to meet her first boyfriend can she identify now? And, with the 70s gone forever, how much of the music and how many of the names can *you* still call to mind?

Whether you think Adam and the Ants are the greatest or you have fond memories of the year *Rock Around the Clock* was released, I hope you have lots of fun with this book – and persuade your friends to buy a copy too.

1

EARLY 60S

QUESTION 1. One point for each correct answer
Who took the following geographical locations into the chart?

1. Red River Rock
2. El Paso
3. Slow Boat to China
4. California Here I Come
5. Caribbean Honeymoon

6. North To Alaska
7. Pasadena
8. Midnight in Moscow
9. Granada
10. 24 Hours From Tulsa

QUESTION 2.
How many instrumentalists/instrumental acts topped the charts between 1960 & 1963?

QUESTION 3.
How much was the prize for winning the stock-car race in Ricky Valance's No. 1 hit 'Tell Laura I Love Her?'

QUESTION 4.
How many pounds of clay were used in the Gene McDaniels/Craig Douglas hit?

QUESTION 5.
How many stars did Richard Chamberlain reckon would 'shine tonight' in his vocal version of the 'Dr. Kildare Theme'?

QUESTION 6.
How old was Neil Sedaka's sweet birthday girl?

QUESTION 7.
How many reasons did Connie Stevens give in 1960?

QUESTION 8.
In April 1962 there were four instrumental T.V. themes in the charts together – can you name them?

QUESTION 9.
In 1961 the T.V. theme Sucu Sucu made the Top 50 via five different acts – can you name them?
(I know 1 measly point each is not much to offer for a mindbending brain stretcher like this, but at least the clever dicks won't get too far ahead!)

QUESTION 10.
The following artists all made their debut in the early 60's. Name their first British hit. 1 point for each.

Del Shannon	*Ronettes*	*Tommy Roe*
Hollies	*Piltdown Men*	

40-50	Get someone to help you collect your prize!
30-40	Go an' get 'em out of the attic and blow the dust off.
20-30	How many did you deliberately get wrong?
10-20	I can lend you a few useful books . . .
0-10	In the words of the Poni-Tails, you were 'Born too late'

3

GUESS WHO?

Own up—how many times have you
had a doodle with the stars,
pencilling in the odd moustache and
dark glasses? Well, you can't do it
with this lot of pictures, 'cause we've
already done it—and sometimes made
even more dramatic changes.
All that's left for you to do is work out
who they are. I was going to caption
them with subtle clues, but that
presented two problems:

1) You lot are too clever, and
2) I'm not subtle—so good luck.

4

WHO IS IT?

The quicker you guess them, the more points you get. Limit yourself to 2 minutes for each one.

QUESTION 1.

 Born in Cambridge

 Originally sang in a duo in another country with Pat Carrol

 Returned to England and joined the group 'Toomorrow'

 1st British hit was a Bob Dylan song in 1971

 The song was 'If not for You'.

Gotcha!

6

QUESTION 2.

 Born in Chicago in 1945

 Recorded as a duo with June Conquest

 Joined Atlantic Records in 1970

 Biggest single success was as 50% of a duo with Roberta Flack in 1972

 It was called 'Where is the Love'

Too late!

QUESTION 3.

 Their lady singer was in the British cast of 'Hair'

 Their album had information about the tracks printed on to the actual record which was innovative at the time.

 They had a big Top 10 single in 1971 on Warner Bros.

 Their violinist/keyboards player was Darryl Way and the drummer was Stewart Copeland.

 O.K. – Here's the give-away for one point – Sonja Kristina was the singer and their hit was 'Back Street Luv'.

Time's up! If I gotcha – Tee Hee! If I didn't, the next one will get you.

 They were formed in Birmingham in February 1966.

 They used to smash T.V. sets on stage, as well as effigies of people they didn't like!

 The opening bars of their first single were based on the '1812 overture'.

 Their 3rd hit was the first record played when Radio 1 opened in September 1967.

 Their leader was Roy Wood.

Flunked again huh? Maybe Brumbeat's not your strong point.

You can make these up for yourself, or you can try this sort of thing–two clues; two different people or groups, but with the same name–who are they?

Give yourselves a couple of points for each one you guess

- *They had a top 20 hit in the summer of 1979 with Space Bass Requiem was the follow up to their 1976 chart topper*

- *She indulged in Pillow Talk in 1973*
  Her Viva Espana was the holiday sing-a-long of 1974

- *Ronnie Wood's group were 'leaving here' in 1965*
  After two top ten hits they turned three times in 1965

GUESS WHO?

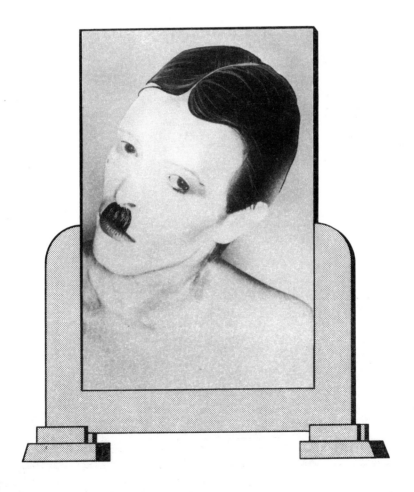

GUESS WHO?

TAMLA MOTOWN

QUESTION 1. A tough one to start with
The Temptations kept the same line up from 1964–1968.
1 point for each member of the group during that period.

QUESTION 2.
Rudolph, Ronald and O'Kelly had hits throughout the
60s and 70s – who are they?

QUESTION 3.
What was the first chart topper on the Tamla Motown
label in the British Charts?

QUESTION 4.
The Four Tops only reached the top once in Britain – with
which song?

QUESTION 5.
Smokey Robinson has had two British No. 1's, one solo –
one with the Miracles. What were they?

12

QUESTION 6.
Diana Ross had a No. 1 with the Supremes in 1964.
What was her next chart topper?

QUESTION 7.
What did Smokey Robinson & The Miracles second?

QUESTION 8.
Where did the Elgins put you?

QUESTION 9.
Where did Shorty Long have a function?

QUESTION 10.
What were Martha & The Vandellas ready for?

QUESTION 11.
What did the Marvellettes' hunter get captured by?

QUESTION 12.
What kind of zoo did the Commodores go to?

QUESTION 13.
How many days in your life did Michael Jackson sing about?

QUESTION 14.
What was in R. Dean Taylor's house?

QUESTION 15.
What did The Isley Brothers hide behind?

QUESTION 16.
What kind of ground were the Temptations standing on?

QUESTION 17.
Who is the boss of Tamla Motown, (now Motown of course)?

QUESTION 18.
When he was going to start the label in 1959, what did he originally want to call it?

QUESTION 19.
Why?

40-50   In the words of The Marvellettes 'You're the one'.

30-40   As The Temptations said about your knowledge, 'It's growing'.

20-30   Ah! so you had some help, well, as Marvin Gaye says – 'It takes two'.

10-20   In the words of Diana Ross – 'I thought it took a little time'.

0-10   You're like The Four Tops – 'Shake Me, Wake Me (when It's Over!)'

GUESS WHO?

GUESS WHO?

For those of you who are regular listeners to the Breakfast Show – you *are* regular listeners to the Breakfast Show, aren't you? – here's a little reminder of a game we played a little while ago. It's not really a quiz, so you can't give yourselves points, but you might have a few laughs – and you can always show off how clever you are by thinking up some more subjects, or making top twenties out of these top tens.

Some of the wacky listeners who sent in this lot were:

David and Barbara Poulton –   *Oaklands, West Midlands*
Mike Fawley – c/o   *Bernard Street, Edinburgh*
Trevor James –   *Castle Lane, Bayston Hill, Shrewsbury, Salop*
Wigan Metro's Land Reclamation Team – (Town Hall, Leigh)
Clive Becksmith –   *The Quay, Conyer, Kent*
Sue and Tony Nelson – Woodside Terrace, Barchory, Aberdeen
Dave Moran –   *Hungerford Road, Edgerton, Huddersfield*
Ken McDonald – Craig Hill, Murray 12, East Kilbride, Scotland
Dave, Calor, Sue –   *Nethercott Close, Luton, Beds*
Kevin –   *Flanders Road, East Ham, London E.6.*
An anonymous listener – The Avenue, West Wickham, Kent
Juliet & Elaine – Manthorpe Estate, Heath Farm, Grantham, Lincs
Bill Renwich – Lichfield Mercury, Bird Street, Lichfield, Staffs
Jane Willmott –   *'Abergeldie', Narnia, Bexhill-on-Sea, Essex.*

– and I've even made up some myself!

BUTTER, MARGARINE, FATS AND CHEESES   TOP TEN

1	**BLUE BAND ON THE RUN** *Wings*	
2	**STORK IN THE MIDDLE WITH YOU** *Stealers Wheel*	
3	**THE TREX OF MY TEARS** *Smokey Robinson and The Miracles*	
4	**CALLING OCCUPANTS OF INTERPLANETARY KRAFT** *Carpenters*	
5	**FLORA YOUR LOVE** *Yardbirds*	
6	**GOUDA TE** *Steeleye Span*	
7	**SUMMER BRIE** *Isley Brothers*	
8	**PHILADELPHIA FREEDOM** *Stilton John*	
9	**I SHOULD HAVE KNOWN CHEDDAR** *Beatles*	
10	**SGT. ROQUEFORT** *X.T.C.*	

GALLUP POLL   TOP TEN

1	**ROCKIN' DOBBIN'** *Michael Jackson*
2	**A LITTLE BIT MORE** *Dr. Hook*
3	**A HORSE WITH NO MANE** *America*
4	**SADDLE BE THE DAY** *Buddy Holly*
5	**FOAL TO CRY** *The Rolling Stones*
6	**COLT TURKEY** *John Lennon*
7	**MAGGIE NEIGH** *Horse Janhowski*
8	**THERE'S A GOAT IN MY HOUSE (Well, some gallop)** *R. Dean Taylor*
9	**FANFARE FOR THE COMMON LAMB (and some gambol)** *E.L.P.*
10	**IT'S GELDING BETTER** *Bridle Ferry*

GUESS WHO?

JOINERS TOP TEN

1	**BITS & BRACES**	*Dave Clark Five*
2	**IF YOU LATHE ME NOW**	*Chicago*
3	**BLOCKBOARD (sawing in the dead of the night)**	*Ron & Russell Nail*
4	**EIGHTEEN WITH A MALLET**	*Pete Wingfield*
5	**HAMMEREUSE**	*Kiki Dee*
6	**DOWELLING BANJOS**	*The Carpenters*
7	**GREAT BALSA FIRE**	*Jerry Lee Lewis*
8	**BEVEL IN DISGUISE**	*Ruler Lenska*
9	**ZIGGY SAWDUST**	*David Bowie*
10	**SPANNERDU**	*Ohio Pliers*

TENNIS TOP TEN

1	**BJORN TO RUN**	*Lobby Siffre*
2	**AND SERVICE IS CHRISTMAS**	*Tennis Waterman*
3	**CAWLEY OCCUPANTS OF INTERPLANETARY CRAFT**	*Ace*
4	**MA HE'S McENROES AT ME**	*Kenny Ball*
5	**GOTFRIED ROCK & ROLL TO YOU**	*Net King Cole*
6	**FOR EVERT IN BLUE JEANS**	*Deuce Newton*
7	**FOR EVER IN BILLIE JEAN'S**	*Frankie Volley & The 4 Seasons*
8	**CONNORSTANTLY**	*Laverace*
9	**(WHAT'S YOUR NAME) VIRGINIA WADE**	*Mottram The Hoople*
10	**THEME FROM S.M.A.S.H.**	*Billie Jean Spears*

GUESS WHO?

GARDENS TOP TEN

1 **I LOVE THE SOUND OF RAKING GRASS**
Patrick Mower

2 **THE SHED'S TOO BIG WITHOUT YOU**
Patio Boulaye

3 **STUCK IN THE MIDDLE WITH YOU**
Stealers Wheelbarrow

4 **MISSTRA MOW-IT-ALL**
Lawny Donegan

5 **TRACKS OF MY SHEARS**
Rakin' Stevens

6 **LIDO SHOVEL**
Leaf Garret

7 **24 FLOWERS FROM TULSA**
Seed Vicious

8 **LAWN HAIRED LOVER FROM LIVERPOOL**
Robert Plant

9 **PAPER HOSES**
Status Hoe

10 **SOME ENCHANTED SEEDLING**
Geno Watering Can & The Ram Jam Band

HI-DE-HI TOP TEN

1 **SMOKE GETS IN YOUR HI-DE-EYES**
Bryan Ferry

2 **THE TIDE IS HI-DE-HI**
Blondie

3 **HI-DE-HO SILVER LINING**
Jeff Beck

4 **HI-DE-LILI HI-DE-LO**
Alan Price Set

5 **RIVER DEEP & MOUNTAIN HI-DE-HI**
Ike & Tina Turner

6 **MA, HE'S MAKIN' HI-DE-HI'S AT ME**
Lena Zavaroni

7 **MICHAEL (ROW THE BOAT ASHORE)**
The Hi-De-Highwaymen

8 **HI-DE-HIGHER GROUND**
Stovie Wonder

9 **HI-HI-HI-DE-HI**
Wings

10 **HI-DE-HI TENSION**
Hi-De-Hi Tension

GUESS WHO?

BIRDS TOP TEN

1 **THIS OLD GROUSE**
Shrikin' Stevens

2 **GIVE GEESE A CHANCE**
The Dove Affair

3 **ANGEL OF THE MOORHEN**
Goose Newton

4 **GULLS, GULLS, GULLS**
Split Hens

5 **TOM HAWK**
Jasper Parrot

6 **TAKE IT TO THE LINNET**
Wren Dodd

7 **LONG HAIRED PLOVER FROM LIVERPOOL**
Owl & Oates

8 **STORKING ON THE MOON**
Squawkwind

9 **FAT BOTTOMED GULLS**
Kite Bush

10 **TOO BUSY THINKIN' 'BOUT MY BUDGIE**
Eider Baker & Arthur Mallard

BATHROOM TOP TEN

1 **TORN BETWEEN TWO LOOFAHS**
Mary McGregor

2 **SOAP ON THE WATER**
Deep Purple

3 **FLUSH**
Queen

4 **SHOWER ME YOU'RE A WOMAN**
Mud

5 **WASHING THE DETECTIVES**
Elvis Costello

6 **BATHING STRANGERS**
Billy Eckstine & Sarah Vaughan

7 **PLUG ME TENDER**
Elvis Presley

8 **TOOTHBRUSH HEAVEN**
The Bee Gees

9 **FLANNELS IN THE RAIN**
The Move

10 **AIN'T GONNA SCRUB NO MORE WITH NO BIG FAT WOMAN**
J.J. Scales

GUESS WHO?

CRICKET TOP TEN

1 **GREAT BAILS OF FIRE**
Jerry Lee Lewis

2 **GOOD GULLEY MISS MOLLY**
Little Richard

3 **I WAS KAISER BILL'S BATSMAN**
Whistling Jack Smith

4 **JESUS CREASE SUPERSTAR**
Murray Head

5 **DO NOT FOUR-SIX ME (OH MY DARLING)**
Frankie Laine

6 **BOTHAM'S BURNING**
Roxy Music

7 **DENNESS TIME**
Cliff Richard

8 **FUNERAL UMPIRE**
The Jam

9 **UNDERARM ROOF**
Rubettes

10 **YOU BATTER YOU BAT**
The Who

DOG TOP TEN

1 **MY OLD MAN'S A DOBERMAN**
Collie Donegan

2 **SPANIEL**
Joe Cocker

3 **POINTER MAN**
Mongrel Jerry

4 **KOOL & THE AFGHAN**
The Korgis

5 **THE BACK OF MY HOUND**
Doggy Osmond

6 **I'M TURNING PEKINESE**
Jimmy Ruffin

7 **I'M A RETRIEVER**
Freddie & The Retrievers

8 **BONE TOO LATE**
The B'Fagles

9 **THE OLDEST SPRINGER IN TOWN**
Spaniel Ballet

10 **WHIPPET**
Brian Poodle & The Tremeloes

RIVERS TOP TEN

1	**FEEL THE TWEED** *Detroit Emeralds*
2	**RIBBLE RIBBLE** *David Bowie*
3	**THE THAMES THEY ARE A-CHANGIN'** *Bob Dylan*
4	**OUSE SORRY NOW** *Connie Francis*
5	**PLEASE DON'T TEES** *Cliff Richard*
6	**WYE** *Anthony Newley*
7	**ARUNAROUND SUE** *Dion*
8	**CAN YOU FEEL THE FORTH?** *Real Thing*
9	**IT'S HARD TO BE HUMBER** *Mac Davis*
10	**NO. 1 SONG IN AVON** *Sparks*

GUESS WHO?

GUESS WHO?

CT DF PK GM

TG iNiTiALS RGH

All of these groups used initials for the titles of one of their records: Can you name them?

Shadows

Abba

Billy Connolly

Joe Tex/Q.Tips

Jackson 5

Bee Gees

Julie Covington etc

Elvis Presley

Village People

Still on initials, how many artists can you think of who use the same initial twice in place of a Christian name?

SONG

One person commences by giving a song title or act and the person next to them has to come up with a song starting with the last letter of the preceding title. 'A' and 'The' should be ignored and there should be a vague time limit i.e. you have to come up with an answer within 10 seconds.

Here's an example doing it with acts:–

BEATLES **S** STATUS QUO **O** OSIBISA **A** AC-DC **C** CILLA BLACK **K** KINKS **S** SLADE **E** ELVIS PRESLEY **Y** YARDBIRDS **S** SHADOWS **S** SIMON & GARFUNKEL **L** LABI SIFFRE **E** ELECTRIC LIGHT ORCHESTRA **A** ALICE COOPER **R** ROCKIN' BERRIES **S** STEALERS WHEEL **L** LOVE SCULPTURE **E** EMERSON

LINKS

and believe it or not, here's an example doing it with songs
(gosh, what a fun book this is):–

GOING UNDERGROUND **D** DOWN THE
DUSTPIPE **E** ELECTRICITY **Y** YESTERDAY **Y**
YOU ARE EVERYTHING **G** GET BACK **K** KIDS
ARE ALRIGHT **T** TRACKS OF MY TEARS **S** SAN
FRANCISCO **O** ON THE ROAD AGAIN **N**
NOBODY DOES IT BETTER **R** ROCK AND ROLL
WALTZ **Z**!

When a player fails to think of an act (or song title) he/she is
eliminated and the eventual winner chooses the next category
– it could mainly be acts or song titles or you might introduce
categories such as T.V. shows, record labels, films, books,
songwriters or anything, depending on where your talents lie.

GUESS WHO?

GROUP TITLES

For one point each, name the group who went with each lead singer:–

Johnny Kidd and the ....

Danny and the ....

Frankie Lymon and the ....

Bobby Angelo and the ....

Billy J. Kramer and the ....

Johnny and the ....

Gladys Knight and the ....

Little Anthony and the...................................

Gary Lewis and the ....

Adam and the ....

? and the ....

ANSWERS PAGE 88

33

GUESS WHO?

Bob Marley and the ....

Terry Dactyl and the ....

Ruby and the ....

Danny Peppermint and the ....

Joey Dee and the ....

Kenny Rogers and the ....

Paul Evans and the ....

Linda and the ....

Smokey Robinson and the ....

Peter Straker and the ....

Maurice Williams and the ....

Larry Cunningham and the ....

Denny Seyton and the ....

Bob B. Soxx and the ....

Harold Melvin and the ....

Freddie Bell and the ....

Moments and ....

Hal Page ....

Eric Burdon and the ....

Cliff Bennett and the ....

Tommy James and the ....

Steve Harley and.......................

ANSWERS PAGE 88

35

GUESS WHO?

Archie Bell and the ....

Geno Washington and the ....

Jimmy James and the ....

Gary Farr and the ....

Linda Carr and the ....

Manuel and his ....

Freddie and the ....

Desmond Decker and the ....

John Fred and the ....

Terry Lightfoot and his ....

Gary Puckett and the ....

Derek and the ....

Eddie Drennon and his ....

Sam the Sham and the ....

Eddie and the ....

Freddie Notes and the ....

Zoot Money and the ....

Dick Charlesworth and his ....

Martha Reeves and the ....

Crispy and ....

Peter Jay and the ....

Brian Poole and the ....

ANSWERS PAGE 8

37

GUESS WHO?

Goldie and the ....

Reperata and the ....

Herb Alpert and the ....

Shane Fenton and the ....

Laurie Lingo and the ....

Emile Ford and the ....

Sly and the ....

Rick Dees and his ....

Bill Haley and the ....

Mike Berry and the ....

Limmie and ....

Adge Cutler and the ....

Nero and the ....

Gerry and the ....

Simon Dupree and the ....

Wayne Fontana and the ....

Disco Tex and the ....

K.C. and the ....

Bette Bright and the....................................

BEATLEMANIA

QUESTION 1.
Abracadabra was a tentative title for which Beatle album?

QUESTION 2.
Who played the mad scientist's assistant Algernon in the Beatles film, 'Help'?

QUESTION 3.
What is the link between the words 'Boy', 'One', 'Prudence' & 'Friend'?

QUESTION 4.
Name the album contining these three tracks
    If I fell
    Tell Me Why
    Any Time At All

QUESTION 5.
Name the album containing these three tracks
    Hey Bulldog
    All Together Now
    Only a Northern Song

QUESTION 6.
Name the album containing these three tracks
    Baby's In Black
    Mr. Moonlight
    Every Little Thing

QUESTION 7.
Name the album containing these three tracks
    Ticket To Ride
    I Need You
    I've Just Seen A Face

QUESTION 8.
Name the album containing these three tracks
    Don't Pass Me By
    Long Long Long
    Goodnight

QUESTION 9. Staggeringly hard (unless you went to Quarry Bank High School).
John Lennon found the Quarrymen in 1955 – 2 pts for any of the seven guys who originally played in the group. You've got 2 pts for a start + a bonus point if you get all 7!

QUESTION 10.
What was the first Beatles hit single?

QUESTION 11.
What was the first individual hit single from John, Paul, George and Ringo?

40-50	**Yeah! Yeah! Yeah!**
30-40	**More fab than most**
20-30	**Not exactly gear but not grotty**
10-20	**You're not destined for a degree in Beatle-ology**
0-10	**No! No! No!**

THE WIRELESS

QUESTION 1 (See over page)

QUESTION 2.
Who was the first ever DJ on Radio One? (Bit tough this one, so here are some clues: he is sensational, owns a barking dog, can never resist removing his shorts during Radio One football matches.

QUESTION 3.
He joined Radio One in 1974 from Radio Luxembourg and had a hit record in 1976: who is he?

QUESTION 4.
He is a softball pitching Oxford graduate who churns out books and plays the piano if pushed: who is he?

QUESTION 5.
A radio programme no longer, it was the Radio One equivalent of Desert Island Discs presented by Brian Matthew. What was it called?

QUESTION 6.
A now defunct Sunday lunch time radio discussion programme hosted by Jimmy Saville.

HOW
DID YOU
SCORE

40-50 Now listen – John Logie Baird worked really hard on that moving picture in a box idea – were his efforts in vain?

30-40 You're the transistor under the bedclothes type, aren't you?

20-30 Only nightshift workers, merchant seamen & tax exiles are excused this disgraceful effort.

10-20 Sentenced to accompany Jimmy Saville O.B.E. on his next Lands End to John O'Groats run.

0-10 You probably have an I.Q. of at least 180, quote long-winded sections of 'War and Peace' to disinterested relatives whilst sliding down plates full of fresh Whitstable oysters and also suffer from gout.

QUESTION 1.
*Gathering of the clans. One point for each of the DJs pictured above.
Possible 25 points (one bonus point if you recognise the guy whose
face is totally obscured).*

44

45

GUESS WHO?

D.J. SONGS

Which Disc Jockeys (past or present), under their real names or pseudonyms, recorded the following songs?

CONVOY G.B.

SO MUCH LOVE

FOOL

CHANTILLY LACE

DISCO DUCK

DISCO SANTA

CAPTAIN KREMMEN

IT ONLY TAKES A MINUTE

MISS YOU

THE FLORAL DANCE

I'll give you 2 points for every one you get wrong!

ANSWERS PAGE 89

47

QUESTION 1
What was the collective name for:–

DANNY, DAVID, BRIAN, SUSAN, SUZANNE,
and SHIRLEY

QUESTION 2
*Who are STELLA, PAUL, HEATHER, MARY
and LINDA*

QUESTION 3
And how were these boys better known:–
MERRILL, JAY, WAYNE, JIMMY, and DONNY
(What a give-away!)

QUESTION 4
From which late 70s song do these lines come?

> *The distant echo of faraway voices
> boarding faraway trains to take them
> home to the ones that they love and
> who love them forever*

THE 70S & 80S

QUESTION 5
And what about this one:–

> *The chances of anything coming from*
> *Mars are a million to one he said*

Into the 80s now – which songs do the following lines come from:–

QUESTION 6
> *You better watch out, you better beware,*
> *Albert said that $E = MC^2$*

QUESTION 7
> *If I get up and dance for you, scream*
> *and shout like a witch will do*

QUESTION 8
> *Well, I'm standing here looking at you*
> *What do I see?*

QUESTION 9
> *Ring! ring! it's seven am*
> *move yourself to go again*

QUESTION 10
> *Back in '68 in a sweaty club*
> *before Jimmy's machine and the rock*
> *steady rub*

GUESS WHO?

One point for each correct answer

QUESTION 1. This one should be appealing!
Name any one hit by these Bells

Archie Bell & The Drells

Freddie Bell & The Bellboys

Maggie Bell

William Bell

QUESTION 2. I Beg Your Parton
Name any one hit by the following charting Partons

David Parton

Stella Parton

Dolly Parton

QUESTION 3. The Prestons'll getcha
Name any one hit by the ensuing Prestons

Billy Preston

Johnny Preston

Mike Preston

QUESTION 4. Starrs in Your Eyes
Name any one hit by these Starrs

Edwin Starr
Freddie Starr
Ringo Starr

QUESTION 5.
Name one hit single from each Stewart

Al Stewart
Billy Stewart
Andy Stewart
Rod Stewart

QUESTION 6.
Name one hit single from each of these Smiths

Patti Smith
Whistling Jack Smith
O.C. Smith
Hurricane Smith

QUESTION 7. The (non Swiss) Family Robinson
Name one hit single from the three Robinsons

Floyd Robinson
Smokey Robinson (solo stuff)
Tom Robinson Band

QUESTION 8. Simple Simons
*Name one hit single (not bored yet are you?) from this tribe
of Simons*

Carly Simon (solo stuff)
Joe Simon
Tito Simon
Paul Simon (solo stuff)

QUESTION 9. Ruffin' it
Name one hit single from the Ruffin trio (no ruffin' now, there's plenty of time)

Bruce Ruffin
David Ruffin
Jimmy Ruffin

QUESTION 10. Great Scott! This one's a toughie, unless you're Simon Scott's niece!
Name one hit single from this lot of Scots

Jack Scott
Linda Scott
Simon Scott

QUESTION 11. (Tinker) Taylor (Soldier Sailor)
Name a hit single by these Taylors

Felice Taylor
James Taylor
Johnny Taylor
R. Dean Taylor

There are lots more glittering stars from the world of showbiz with similar names – what fun to find some more eh! No? Oh well, you could always finish off this week's Beano and then return refreshed to this literary masterpiece.

BEAT THE JOCK
PAPER ONE
Time limit – 15 minutes

*Answer **all** the questions, or at least some of them.*

*Number your answers fully in the left-hand margin (or in the right-hand margin), e.g. **1, 2,** etc.*

*Leave a space of at least **three** lines after your completed answer to each **whole** question.*

*You should attempt **all** the questions if you want, but marks will be given only for your best **seven** answers, if at all.*

QUESTION 1
From which towns do the following groups originate?

Slade	Piranhas
Moody Blues	Undertones
Troggs	Angelic Upstart
Hollies	Specials
Teardrop Explodes	Dr. Feelgood

54

QUESTION 2
In terms of weeks spent in the chart, who were the champions of the following years?

1975
Bay City Rollers, Showaddywaddy or Mud

1978
*John Travolta & Olivia Newton-John,
Bee Gees or Boney M*

1967
Beatles, Engelbert Humperdinck, Procol Harum

1971
T. Rex, Elvis Presley or Sweet

1962
Acker Bilk, The Tornados, The Shadows

QUESTION 3
Seven Eurovision songs have made No. 1 in Britain – can you name them?

QUESTION 4
Name three acts who have had British hits with the song "Tell Him".

QUESTION 5
What is the conservation link between:–

Judy Collins; Country Joe McDonald; David Crosby and Graham Nash; Mike McGear

QUESTION 6
Name any Kinks album that had a theme running through it.

GUESS WHO?

QUESTION 7
Here are the titles of some pop films –
– name the year

Ferry Cross the Mersey
Help
The Girls on the Beach

Mad Dogs and Englishmen
200 Motels
Rainbow Bridge

Stardust
Tommy
Janis

The Blue Bros
Coal Miner's Daughter
No Nukes

The Wiz
Sgt. Pepper's Lonely Heart Club Band
American Hot Wax

GUESS WHO?

BEAT THE JOCK
PAPER TWO
CONNECTIONS

This one's for clever dicks and smarty pants. The first person asks a pop music question and the next question has to retain a link with the answer.

QUESTION 1
Who's the only person to have had a hit with Johnny B. Goode?

QUESTION 2
His middle name was the same as half of the duo who had a top ten hit in 1978.

QUESTION 3
Some one else behaved like that duo but they did it in the street.

QUESTION 4
That lead singer's name is the same as one of the Beatles' pets, sung about on which album?

QUESTION 5
The previous album's title was the same as a big 70s soul/disco singer. What was the chart success?

QUESTION 6
Half the Orchestra's title is the same as a mid/late 60s American group – who was their front man?

QUESTION 7
A singer who had the same Christian name as Mr. Love had a no. 1 hit in 1968 – what was it called?

QUESTION 8

Add some rain to the previous answer and it becomes a hit for its writer – who is it?

QUESTION 9

A guy with the same surname had a number one American hit in 1976 with Disco Lady

QUESTION 10

In 1980 a couple from Gundaloupe really spelled out half of the previous singer's American number one. Who were they?

BEAT THE JOCK
PAPER THREE
TIME FACTORS

Here's something else you can improve on for yourselves. Give yourself – or each person if you're playing with friends – a time limit, say two minutes, and see how many song titles you can think of with a certain theme.

For example, how many hit songs can you think of with colours in the title? How many people's names? Numbers? Place names?

I've given a couple of examples on page 90 (I know *you* won't need them but *they* insisted), you'll be able to come up with lots. And you can invent more categorics or broaden your scope. How many instrumental hits can you name? How many groups or artists beginning with a given letter of the alphabet (whoever gets most nominates the next letter) – you could write a book about it.

BEAT THE JOCK
PAPER FOUR

Yet another idea you can work on (after all, I've made up most of the questions – it's time you had a go).

One person nominates a year, and the others have to write down as many No. 1's as they can from that year. The winner then nominates another year, and so on. The proposer acts as timekeeper. It's best to decide on your own time limit depending on the skill of the participants and the difficulty of the year.

(The list of chart topping singles 1952-1980 can be found in the Guinness Book of British Hit Singles).

GUESS WHO?

GUESS WHO?

GUESS WHO?

QUESTION 1 (For animal lovers)
They had just one more night in 1978

QUESTION 2
From Holland they took a principal American river to the top

QUESTION 3
Their first of three Top Twenty hits was in Black & White

QUESTION 4 (For food lovers)
They made it with you in 1970

64

QUESTION 5
He became dizzy in 1969

QUESTION 6
Their first hit came in wrapping paper

QUESTION 7 (Sport's the link between the next 3 questions)
They had a touch too much in 1974

QUESTION 8
They had a hat-trick of No.2 records in 1978

QUESTION 9
*They had hits in the late 50s and early 60s
both with and without their late lead singer.*

QUESTION 10 (Name these artists – with a colour
connection
He was a lonely boy in 1977

QUESTION 11
*He was tired of being alone in 1971 and decided to
stay together in 1972*

QUESTION 12
They got up and boogied in 1976

*Make more of these up yourself – there are lots
of 'em, and you can think up more categories to
test your chums.*

65

GUESS WHO?

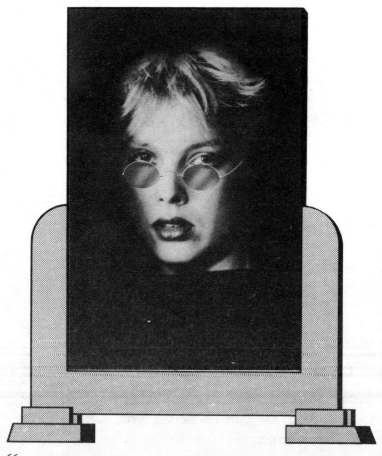

DANCE STANCE

How many songs that got to Number One actually included the name of a dance? To get all of these you'll probably have to track down dad out in the garage or pop round to granny's house and gently nudge the recollections of her halcyon days.

To help you out, here are the artists and the years.

1955	Rosemary Clooney
1955	Bill Haley and the Comets
1950	Kay Starr
1958	Elvis Presley
1962	Elvis Presley
1967	Engelbert Humperdinck
1973	Wizzard
1974	George McRae
1977	Baccara
1979	Specials

If you're desperately clever, you could see who can get the most in 30 seconds or 1 minute – not necessarily number ones.

e.g. Alma Cogan – *Never do a Tango with an Eskimo*
Swinging Blue Jeans – *Hippy Hippy Shake*
Van McCoy – *The Hustle*

and of course there have been dozens and dozens of weird dances hastily constructed out of necessity over the years – loads of extra points if you can remember who you danced with at the time (or didn't have the courage to)!

1960/61

Can you work out these song titles?
2 points each. I've done the first one
to show you what I'm on about:–

QUESTION 1
Moving Verse (Poetry in Motion by Johnny Tillotson)

QUESTION 2
Leave the South for a territory the U.S.A. bought
from Russia in 1868

QUESTION 3
Gun Toting Mother

QUESTION 4
Mr. D.I.Y.

QUESTION 5
Nearly full marks

QUESTION 6
An insect with a beard, sloppy pullover and sandals

QUESTION 7
Romantic Cot

QUESTION 8
Not moving on the junction of two streets

QUESTION 9
Painful posterior

QUESTION 10
Bein' good

QUESTION 1
Jolly Tar?

QUESTION 2
Riding up and down on the fairground

QUESTION 3
Marionette on a small piece of rope

QUESTION 4
An underground tragedy from 26 years before

QUESTION 5
All right or two letters of the alphabet

QUESTION 6
James Bond

QUESTION 7
A funny man expires

QUESTION 8
The 12 o'clock lights on fire

QUESTION 9
Partly worn out boot

QUESTION 10
Mirrored Images

Mid-70s

QUESTION 1
At liberty in an American state

QUESTION 2
Chattering Vegetation

QUESTION 3
Come of age with ammunition

QUESTION 4
Expensive Sweetener

QUESTION 5
Hire St. Nick

QUESTION 6
Accordion

QUESTION 7
It's O.K., It's Free

QUESTION 8
An Upset Dessert

QUESTION 9
Shelf? . . . Breakfast?

QUESTION 10
Return to CCCP

1977/78

QUESTION 1
Where they make bread in the road

QUESTION 2
Copying one another

QUESTION 3
Blocking the radio

QUESTION 4
A command from the Abbot to the Monks during prayers

QUESTION 5
Could also be the letter 'O'

QUESTION 6
Cairo Ska

QUESTION 7
Solar Vacations

QUESTION 8
All three are tidy

QUESTION 9
Ray Thomas or Graham Edge

QUESTION 10
A smashing penchant

GUESS WHO?

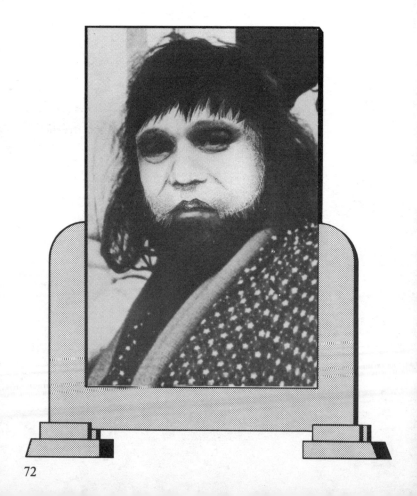

GUESS WHO?

1978

QUESTION 1
A small amount of cleansing agent

QUESTION 2
Stand-in

QUESTION 3
Initially it's a hostel

QUESTION 4
Perspiring during the darkest hours

QUESTION 5
Unclean heavenly bodies

QUESTION 6
Colourful drink

QUESTION 7
Gentleman up above on a sunny day

QUESTION 8
300 seconds

QUESTION 9
Firing a planet

QUESTION 10
Person who hails from America's most famous East coast city

Elvis

QUESTION 1
Tear it to shreds

QUESTION 2
Mistrust

QUESTION 3
Three part song from the States

QUESTION 4
Blue grass precipitation

QUESTION 5
Relentlessly pursue a four-legged friend

QUESTION 6
American guy

QUESTION 7
Neither tamed not in the city

QUESTION 8
Notes expressing feelings from the heart

QUESTION 9
Relative passion

QUESTION 10
Given word on real estate

GUESS WHO?

GUESS WHO?

Beatles

QUESTION 1
Retreat

QUESTION 2
Agatha Christie

QUESTION 3
Native of the country that got no points in the Eurovision contest – probably will

QUESTION 4
Musicians from a seasonal three-striped institution

QUESTION 5
A colour that runs deep

QUESTION 6
A copper road

QUESTION 7
Stumble every 24 hours

QUESTION 8
Airborne

QUESTION 9
S.O.S.

QUESTION 10
Oh! I nearly forgot these three little words.

Cliff

QUESTION 1
A colour becomes another

QUESTION 2
Charmed part of the face

QUESTION 3
Out of town

QUESTION 4
Blow up

QUESTION 5
Several of us agree

QUESTION 6
Refrain from taking the micky

QUESTION 7
Nearly every time

QUESTION 8
All the time

QUESTION 9
The all clear

QUESTION 10
Q.E.2.

EUROVISION

QUESTION 1

Which country obtained no points at all in both the 1980 & 81 contest?

QUESTION 2.

Which year was there a four way tie for first place which included the British entry sung by Lulu?

QUESTION 3.

Cliff Richard has represented Britain twice in the Eurovision – 1968 & 1973. What were the songs?

QUESTION 4.
*Britain won the Eurovision four times in
1967/1969/1976/1981. Who represented us?*

QUESTION 5.
*Ireland have won the contest twice – in 1970 and 1980.
Who sang the winning songs?*

QUESTION 6.
Who sang the following British Eurovision entries?
> *Beg, Steal or Borrow*
> *Rock Bottom*
> *Are You Sure*
> *Love Enough for Two*

QUESTION 7.
*Israel won the Eurovision 1978 & 1979. Lots of generous
points – 4 each – for naming the songs and the artists.
Plus bonus 4 pts for completely correct spelling (getting
sneaky now!)*

40-50	You're either Cliff Richard, Sandie Shaw, Olivia Newton-John or one of Bucks Fizz
30-40	You're bi-lingual or you cheated
20-30	You still know too much about it
10-20	That's better – you can hold your head up in company
0-10	Well done! You can feel justifiably proud.

CRYPTIC QUIZ

Tamla Motown

QUESTION 1
A coat called James
QUESTION 2
A definite occurrence
QUESTION 3
Somewhere it doesn't rain
QUESTION 4
It's difficult to understand this grand dance
QUESTION 5
Take you time before buying
QUESTION 6
Could be said of Hank Marvin, Bruce Welch or Brian Bennett
QUESTION 7
Seating arrangements on a tandem
QUESTION 8
Recently
QUESTION 9
Off to the discotheque
QUESTION 10
I agree with your feeling

If you're organising some of these quizzes yourself, the following books are pretty useful (expensive, but useful).

The Guinness Book of British Hit Singles
by
Jo and Tim Rice, Paul Gambaccini and Mike Read

Lillian Moxon's Rock Encyclopedia
compiled by Ed Naha

British Record Charts 1955-1979
by
Tony Jasper

The Guinness Book of Hits of the 70s
by
Jo and Tim Rice, Paul Gambaccini and Mike Read

Rock Family Trees
by
Pete Frame

Encyclopedia of British Beat Groups and Solo Artists of the 60s
Colin Cross, Paul Kendall and Mick Farren

N.M.E. Encyclopedia of Rock
Nick Logan and Bob Wolfinden

The Book of Golden Discs
Joseph Murrells

25 Years of Rock
John Tobler, BBC

DID YOU GUESS?

Wreckless Eric

Glen Campbell

Tho Vopors

Royer Taylor of Uueen

Matchbox

The Knack

Paul McCartney

Rolling Stones

Ten Pole Tudor

Duran Duran

Talking Heads

85

Billy Idol

Frankie Valli

Neil Young

John Lydon

Captain Beefheart

Frank Sinatra

David Bowie

Dave Dee

The Motors

Wings

Kate Bush

Paul Burnett

Arlo Guthrie

Sheena Easton

Nash The Slash

Demis Roussos

Kim Wilde

Phil Collins

Jona Lewie

The Jam

The Action

Japan

ANSWERS

Early 60s
Q.1. Johnny and the Hurricanes/Marty Robbins/Emile Ford/Freddy Cannon/Frank Weir/Johnny Horton/Temperance 7/ Kenny Ball/Frank Sinatra/Gene Pitney

Q.2. The Shadows: 5 Times (Apache/Kon Tiki/Wonderful Land/Dance On/Foot Tapper)
Floyd Kramer (On the Rebound)
B. Bumble and the Stingers (Nut Rocker)
Tornados (Telstar)
Jet Harris and Tony Meehan (Diamonds)

Q.3. $1000

Q.4. 100

Q.5. 3

Q.6. 16

Q.7. 16

Q.8. Theme from Z Cars/Dr. Kildare Theme/The Maigret Theme/Strangers on the Shore

Q.9. Laurie Johnson/Ted Heath/Nina and Frederick/Ping Ping and Al Verclane/Joe Loss

Q.10. Del Shannon- Runaway (1961)
Hollies–Just Like Me (1963)
Ronettes–Be My Baby (1963)
Piltdown Men–MacDonalds Cave (1960)
Tommy Roe–Sheila (1962)

Who Is It?
Q.1. Olivia Newton-John

Q.2. The late Donnie Hathaway

Q.3. Curved Air

Q.4. The Move
If you did well you're entitled to the letters M.O.V.E. after your name – Meritorious Order of Valiant Effort
● Slick/Slik; Sylvia/Sylvia (two different people, honest!);
The Birds/The Byrds

Tamla Motown
Q.1. Otis Williams, David Ruffin, Eddie Kendricks, Melvin Franklin and Paul Williams

Q.2. The Isley Brothers

Q.3. Baby Love by The Supremes (1964)

Q.4. Reach Out, I'll Be There (1966)

Q.5. Being With You (1981), Tears of a Clown (1970)

Q.6. I'm Still Waiting (1971)

Q.7. That Emotion

Q.8. In My Place

Q.9. At the Junction

Q.10. Love

Q.11. The Game

Q.12. The Human Zoo

Q.13. One

Q.14. A Ghost

Q.15. A Painted Smile

Q.16. Shaky Ground

Q.17. Berry Gordy Jr.

Q.18. Tammy

Q.19. After Debbie Reynolds' 1957 hit.

Initials
F.B.I./S.O.S./D.I.V.O.R.C.E./S.Y.S.L.J.F.M./A.B.C./I.O.I.O./O.K.
T.R.O.U.B.L.E./Y.M.C.A.

P.P. Arnold/B.B. King/J.J. Barrie/J.J. Cale/Z.Z. Top

Group Titles
Johnny Kidd and the Pirates
Danny and the Juniors
Frankie Lymon and the Teenagers
Bobby Angelo and the Tuxedos
Billy J. Kramer and the Dakotas
Johnny and the Hurricanes
Gladys Knight and the Pips
Little Anthony and the Imperials
Gary Lewis and the Playboys
Adam and the Ants
? and the Mysterians
Bob Marley and the Wailers
Terry Dactyl and the Dinosaurs
Ruby and the Romantics
Danny Peppermint and the Jumping Jacks
Joey Dee and the Starliters
Kenny Rogers and the First Edition
Paul Evans and the Curls
Linda and the Funky Boys
Smokey Robinson and the Miracles
Peter Straker and the Hands of Dr. Teleny
Maurice Williams and the Zodiacs
Larry Cunningham and the Mighty Avons
Denny Seyton and the Sabres
Bob B. Soxx and the Blue Jeans
Harold Melvin and the Blue Notes
Freddie Bell and the Bell Boys
Moments and Whatnauts
Hal Page and the Whalers
Eric Burdon and the Animals
Cliff Bennett and the Rebel Rousers
Tommy James and the Shondells
Steve Harley and Cockney Rebel
Archie Bell and the Drells
Geno Washington and the Ram Jam Band
Jimmy James and the Vagabonds
Gary Farr and the T. Bones
Linda Carr and the Love Squad
Manuel and his Music of the Mountains
Freddie and the Dreamers
Desmond Dekker and the Aces
John Fred and the Playboy Band
Terry Lightfoot and his New Orleans Jazzmen
Gary Puckett and the Union Gap
Derek and the Dominoes
Eddie Drennon and BBS Unlimited
Sam the Sham and the Pharaohs
Eddie and the Hot Rods
Freddie Notes and the Rudies
Zoot Money and the Big Roll Band
Dick Charlesworth and his City Gents
Martha Reeves and the Vandellas
Crispy and Company
Peter Jay and the Jaywalkers
Brian Poole and the Tremeloes
Goldie and the Gingerbreads
Reparata and the Delrons
Herb Alpert and the Tijuana Brass
Shane Fenton and the Fentones
Laurie Lingo and the Dipsticks
Emile Ford and the Checkmates
Sly and the Family Stone
Rick Dees and his Cast of Idiots
Bill Haley and the Comets
Mike Berry and the Outlaws
Limmie and Family Cookin'
Adge Cutler and the Wurzels
Nero and the Gladiators
Gerry and the Pacemakers
Simon Dupree and the Big Sound
Wayne Fontana and the Mindbenders
Disco Tex and the Sex-O-Lettes
K.C. and the Sunshine Band
Bette Bright and the Illuminations

Beatlemania

Q.1. Revolver

Q.2. Roy Kinnear

Q.3. They are all Beatle songs prefixed by the word *Dear*:
Dear Boy (From Paul McCartney's Ram Album); Dear One
(George Harrison's 33⅓ Album); Dear Prudence (Beatles White
Album); Dear Friend (Wings Wild Life Album)

Q.4. A Hard Day's Night

Q.5. Yellow Submarine

Q.6. Bealtes For Sale

Q.7. Help

Q.8. The Beatles White Album

Q.9. John Lennon, Pete Shotton, Colin Hanton, Rodney Davis,
Nigel Whalley, Eric Griffiths, Len Garry

Q.10. Love Me Do (1962)

Q.11. John–Give Peace A Chance (1969) Ringo–It Don't Come
Easy (1971) Paul–Another Day (1971) George–My Sweet Lord
(1971)

The Wireless

Q.1.

1. Dave Cash
2. Ed Stewart
3. Noel Edmonds
4. Pete Murray
5. Duncan Johnson
6. Richard Skinner
7. Pete Drummond
8. Andy Peebles
9. Mike Read
10. Tony Prince
11. Steve Wright
12. Dave Lee Travis
13. Tommy Vance
14. Anne Nightingale
15. Simon Bates
16. Keith Skues
17. Johnny Moran
18. David Jacobs
19. Paul Burnett
20. Peter Powell
21. Tony Blackburn
22. Stuart Henry
23. Rob Jones
24. Alan Freeman

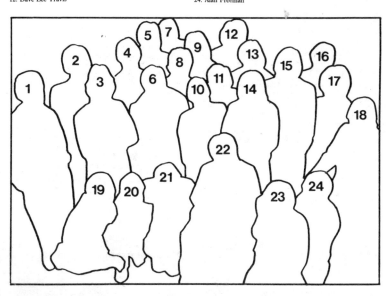

Q.2. Tony Blackburn

Q.3. Paul Burnett (Half of Laurie Lingo and the Dipsticks)

Q.4. Paul Gambaccini

Q.5. My Top Twelve

Q.6. Speakeasy

D.J. Songs

Dave Lee Travis and Paul Burnett as Laurie Lingo and the
Dipsticks/Tony Blackburn/Al Mathews/The Big Bopper
(J.P. Richardson)/Rick Dees/Chris Hill/Kenny Everett/Jonathan
King as One Hundred Ton and a Feather/Jimmy Young/
Terry Wogan

The 70s and 80s

Q.1. The Partridge Family (not a real family folks)

Q.2. The McCartney Family

Q.3. The Osmonds

Q.4. Down in the Tube Station at Midnight (The Jam; words and music by Paul Weller, published by And Son Music Ltd)

Q.5. Eve of the War (from Jeff Wayne's War of the Worlds, published by April/Jeff Wayne Music)

Q.6. Einstein A Go-go (Landscape; words and music by John Walters, Richard Burgess and Landscape, published by Event Horizon)

Q.7. Attention to Me (The Nolans; words and music by Findon/Myers/Puzey published by Black Sheep Music)

Q.8. Ant Music (Adam and the Ants; words and music by Ant/Peroni, published by EMI)

Q.9. Magnificent Seven (The Clash; words and music by Mick Jones/Joe Strummer, published by Nineden)

Q.10 Geno (Dexy's Midnight Runners; words and music by Rowland/Archer published by EMI)

The Name's the Same

Q.1. Archie–Here I Go Again/There's Gonna Be A Showdown/Soul City Walk/Everybody Have A Good Time
Freddie–Giddy-up-a-ding-dong
Maggie–Hazel
William–Tribute to a King/Private Number (with Judy Clay)

Q.2. David–Isn't She Lovely
Stella–The Danger of a Stranger
Dolly–Jolene

Q.3. Billy–That's the Way God Planned It/Outa Space
Johnny–Running Bear/Cradle of Love/I'm Starting To Go Steady/Feel So Fine/Charming Billy
Mike–Mr. Blue/I'll Do Anything/Togetherness/Marry Me

Q.4. Edwin–Stop Her On Sight/Headline News/Twenty Five Miles/War/Stop The War Now
Freddie–It's You/White Christmas
Ringo–It Don't Come Easy/Back Off Boogaloo/Photograph/You're Sixteen/Only You

Q.5. Al–Year of the Cat
Billy–Summertime
Andy–Donald Where's Your Troosers/A Scottish Soldier/The Battle's O'er/Dr. Finlay
Rod–Oh lot's of them, I'm terribly lazy and I'm sure you're right

Q.6. Patti–Because The Night/Privilege (Set Me Free)
Whistling Jack–I Was Kaiser Bill's Batman
O.C.–Son of Hickory Hollers Tramp/Together
Hurricane–Don't Let It Die/Oh Babe What Would You Say/Who Was It

Q.7. Floyd– Makin' Love
Smokey–Just My Soul Responding/Being With You
Tom–2-4-6-8 Motorway/Don't Take No For an Answer/Up Against the Wall/Bully for You

Q.8. Carly– You're So Vain/The Right Thing To Do/Nobody Does It Better
Joe–Step By Step
Tito–This Monday Morning Feeling
Paul–Me and Julio Down By The Schoolyard/Mother and Child Reunion/Take Me To The Mardi Gras/Loves Me Like A Rock/50 Ways to Leave Your Lover/Slip Slidin' Away

Q.9. Bruce–Rain/Mad About You
David–Walk Away From Love
Jimmy– What Becomes of the Broken Hearted/I've Passed This Way Before/Gonna Give Her All The Love I've Got/Farewell Is A Lonely Sound/I'll Say Forever My Love/It's Wonderful/Tell Me What You Want

Q.10. Jack–My True Love/The Way I Walk/What In The World's Come Over You/Burning Bridges
Linda–I've Told Every Little Star/Don't Eat Meaty Honey
Simon–Move It Baby

Q.11. Felice–I Feel Love Coming On
James–Fire and Rain/You've Got A Friend
Johnny–Disco Lady
R. Dean–Gotta See Jane/Indiana Wants Me/There's A Ghost In My House/Window Shopping

Beat The Jock

Q.1. Slade– Wolverhampton; Moody Blues–Birmingham; Troggs–Andover; Hollies–Manchester; Teardrop Explodes–Liverpool; Piranhas–Brighton; Undertones–Londonderry; Angelic Upstart–Newcastle; Specials–Coventry; Dr. Feelgood–Southend

Q.2. 1975 Mud 45 weeks to the Rollers' 31 and Showaddywaddy's 36
1978 Boney M 54 weeks to the Bee Gee's 51 and John Travolta & Olivia Newton-John's 42
1967 Engelbert 96 weeks to The Beatles' 30 and Procol Harum's 25
1971 Elvis 66; T. Rex 47 and Sweet 34
1962 Acker Bilk 71; The Shadows 38 and the Tornados 17

Q.3. Puppet on a String–Sandie Shaw (1967)
Congratulations–Cliff Richard (1968)
All Kinds of Everything–Dana (1970)
Waterloo–Abba (1974)
Save Your Kisses For Me–Brotherhood of Man (1976)
What's Another Year–Johnny Logan (1980)
Making Your Mind Up–Bucks Fizz (1981)

Q.4. Billie Davis (1963), The Exciters (1963) and Hello (1974)

Q.5. They've all recorded songs about whales:
Judy Collins–Farewell to Tarwathie
Country Joe–Little Blue Whale and Save The Whales
Crosby and Nash–To The Last Whale
Mike McGear–Save the Whale

Q.6. Arthur/A Soap Opera/Village Green Preservation Society

Q.7. 1965/1971/1974/1980/1978

Beat The Jock 2

Q.1. Jimi Hendrix (middle name Marshall)

Q.2. Marshall Hain

Q.3. Martha Reeves and the Vandellas (Dancing in the Street)

Q.4. The White Album (Martha My Dear–Martha was Paul McCartney's dog)

Q.5. Love Unlimited Orchestra (Barry White)

Q.6. Arthur Lee (the group was Love)

Q.7. Fire (Arthur Brown)

Q.8. James Taylor (Fire and Rain)

Q.9. Johnnie Taylor

Q.10. Ottawan (D.I.S.C.O.)

Beat The Jock 3

Colours: Little Red Rooster (Rolling Stones); Black is Black (Los Bravos)
Numbers: 634-5789 (Wilson Pickett); It Takes Two (Marvin Gaye and Kim Weston)
Names: Peggy Sue (Buddy Holly); Jolly Roger (Adam and the Ants)
Places: I Don't Wanna Go To Chelsea (Elvis Costello); Winchester Cathedral (New Vaudeville Band)

Coming Apart At The Themes

Q.1. Yellow Dog

Q.2. Pussycat

Q.3. Greyhound

Q.4. Bread

Q.5. Tommy Roe

Q.6. Cream

Q.7. Arrows

Q.8. Darts

Q.9. Crickets

Q.10 Andrew Gold

Q.11. Al Green

Q.12. Silver Convention

Dance Stance

The songs were Mambo Italiano; Rock Around The Clock; Rock and Roll Waltz; Jailhouse Rock; Rock a Hula Baby; The Last Waltz; See My Baby Jive; Rock Your Baby; Yes Sir, I Can Boogie; Skinhead Moon Stomp (part of live E.P.)

I reckon the word 'Rock' is fair enough for a dance as in C'mon Let's Rock. 'Boogie', I suppose is debatable. But just think how much fun you can have moaning about how unfair the whole stupid question was!

Cryptic Quiz

1960-61

Q.1. We helped you out with this one, remember?
Q.2. North to Alaska (Johnny Horton)
Q.3. Pistol Packin' Mama (Gene Vincent)
Q.4. Handy Man (Jimmy Jones)
Q.5. Nine Times Out Of Ten (Cliff Richard)
Q.6. Beatnik Fly (Johnny and the Hurricanes)
Q.7. Cradle of Love (Johnny Preston)
Q.8. Standing on the Corner (King Brothers)
Q.9. Rawhide (Frankie Laine)
Q.10. Ain't Misbehavin' (Tommy Bruce)

1967

Q.1. Happy Jack (The Who)
Q.2. On A Carousel (The Hollies)
Q.3. Puppet On A String (Sandie Shaw)
Q.4. New York Mining Disaster 1941 (Bee Gees)
Q.5. Okay (Dave Dee Dozy Beaky Mick and Tich)
Q.6. OO7 (Desmond Dekker)
Q.7. Death of a Clown (Dave Davies)
Q.8. Burning of the Midnight Lamp (Jimi Hendrix)
Q.9. Hole in My Shoe (Traffic)
Q.10. Reflections (Diana Ross and the Supremes)

Mid-70s

Q.1. Philadelphia Freedom (Elton John)
Q.2. Whispering Grass (Windsor Davies and Don Estelle)
Q.3. Eighteen with a Bullet (Pete Wingfield)
Q.4. Money Honey (Bay City Rollers)
Q.5. Renta Santa (Chris Hill)
Q.6. Squeeze Box (The Who)
Q.7. No Charge (J.J. Barrie)
Q.8. Fool To Cry (Rolling Stones)
Q.9. Continental (Maureen McGovern)
Q.10. Back in the USSR (Beatles)

1977-78

Q.1. Baker Street (Gerry Rafferty)
Q.2. Follow You, Follow Me (Genesis)
Q.3. Jamming (Bob Marley)
Q.4. Let's All Chant (Michael Zager)
Q.5. Figaro (Brotherhood of Man)
Q.6. Egyptian Reggae (Jonathan Richman)
Q.7. Holidays in the Sun (Sex Pistols)
Q.8. Neat Neat Neat (The Damned)
Q.9. Moody Blue (Elvis Presley)
Q.10 I Love The Sound of Breaking Glass (Nick Lowe)

1978

Q.1. A Little Bit of Soap (Showaddywaddy)
Q.2. Substitute (Clout)
Q.3. Y.M.C.A. (Village People)
Q.4. Night Fever (Bee Gees)
Q.5. Angels With Dirty Faces (Sham 69)
Q.6. Lilac Wine (Elkie Brooks)

Q.7. Mr. Blue Sky (E.L.O.)
Q.8. Five Minutes (The Stranglers)
Q.9. Shooting Star (Dollar)
Q.10. Native New Yorker (Odyssey)

Elvis

Q.1. Rip It Up
Q.2. Suspicion
Q.3. American Trilogy
Q.4. Kentucky Rain
Q.5. Hound Dog
Q.6. U.S. Male
Q.7. Wild In The Country
Q.8. Love Letters
Q.9. Kissin' Cousins
Q.10. Promised Land

Beatles

Q.1. Get Back
Q.2. Paperback Writer
Q.3. Norwegian Wood
Q.4. Sergeant Pepper's Lonely Hearts Club Band
Q.5. Yellow Submarine
Q.6. Penny Lane
Q.7. Day Tripper
Q.8. Flying
Q.9. Help
Q.10. P.S. I Love You

Cliff

Q.1. When Blue Turns To Grey
Q.1. Lucky Lips
Q.3. In The Country
Q.4. Dynamite
Q.5. We Say Yeah
Q.6. Please Don't Tease
Q.7. 9 times out of 10
Q.8. Constantly
Q.9. Green Light
Q.10. Big Ship

Eurovision

Q.1. Norway
Q.2. 1969 (Between U.K./France/Spain/Holland)
Q.3. Congratulations and Power To All Our Friends
Q.4. Sandie Shaw/Lulu/Brotherhood of Man/Bucks Fizz
Q.5. Dana and Johnnie Logan
Q.6. The New Seekers (1972) / Lynsey de Paul and Mike Moran (1977) / The Allisons (1961) / Prima Donna (1980)
Q.7. Izhar Cohen and Alphabeta singing A Ba Ni Bi (1978) / Milk and Honey singing Hallelujah (1979)

Cryptic Quiz

Tamla Motown

Q.1. Jimmy Mack (Martha and the Vandellas)
Q.2. The Happening (The Supremes)
Q.3. A Place in the Sun (Stevie Wonder)
Q.4. Ball of Confusion (The Temptations)
Q.5. Shop Around (The Miracles)
Q.6. Standing In The Shadows (The Four Tops)
Q.7. It Takes Two (Marvin Gaye and Kim Weston)
Q.8. Lately (Stevie Wonder)
Q.9. Going To Go-go (The Miracles)
Q.10. I Second That Emotion (Smokey Robinson and the Miracles)